I0435722

CONNECTIONS MAGAZINE
CM. Monthly Review. In this
issue:

Different source make really big difference. Never too late to shed couple of inches . What is it? Inside this issue, you discover lot more...............Southern California This Weekend...Hot Topics too

Take advantage of special offer

It is about people, life style,

and the struggle
On sale at amazon.com

to settle for equal or better

values.

Shop weconnect2.com online store

proper attire
Fashion statement for everyone. make it sound.
Are you listed in our business directory . it is the best.
International Business of many great names.
WECONNECT2 BUSINESS DIRECTORY.

(We Connect 2)

popular web at weconnect2.com..Learn more, Varsity,
and "Be The Best" you can be.

The Connections, this summer issue, a publication brought to you in part by weconnect2.com online news and media publishing . Selective and hot topics, related article and if we do not cover it you get it custom delivered from Google as our back up in your search.

Communities work force

Diversity

news for traveling

visitsoutherncalifornia.net

News U.S Journal..online nusjournal.com we deliver the best,you might find everything elsewhere.
It is online news and media monitor, in Souther California hot spots, and anywhere else in the world.
simple, visit and subscribe the easy way. Just leave your e-mail

address.

-Connecting the neighborhood, and the communities to the world.

Support Your Community:
"Shop Here" on flying flags hanging on the out skirt of the town, you see more on the stores windows, to keep the community stronger, more promotions of patriotic sound such as "support your local merchants", and "eat fresh made here" . The idea to further encourage the residents to continue closer shopping to home and making their money as an investment toward a better life style by making sure more of their cash flow stream through their own community channels.

London based economic think tank, The New Economics Foundation, in a research comparing buying from outside of the community or from a large supermarket VS buying local and from family owned so called pop and mom shop stores, the results indicate a strong money flow toward the local stores almost twice as much in value for both local merchants and the community residents shoppers.

THE INTERNATIONAL ASSOCIATION OF STUDENTS IN BUSINESS AND

ECONOMICS

(Be part of the experience, or refer someone. AIESEC provide on hands experience for graduating college students just about anywhere in the world. It is to exchange one for one internships world wide.)

Local products at best is for sure the number one provided by most members of the community is "Customer Service". The least to say one would have of high quality and best value for their money. If provided, raw materials to produce everything local will make life much easier and the community very strong economically and self resilience.

good health plan hard to find

Self reliance is aimed with embitous for anyone when it is possible. But far from self reliance, is an open market when promoting local shopping. Most of the products are paid for by the locals both merchants and residents after delivery. From the gasoline pump to the brewed drip or else when last time both met at anyone backyard.

Educating the public and in specific members of the local community both residents and official representative is very crucial in keeping the community in stable status and for better and stronger future. Not by going to school and obtaining degrees to work for companies everywhere else, by educating the shoppers and merchants on those issues that most of the product are from else where anyway paid for already by the locals, for example soap, and bread, and most of the produce as ingredients in any food prepared items.

Stable communities have build many years of economic stability in cities where they belong, also for years to come. In other than small town more than few communities exist in a city for example:

In the City of Los Angeles often spoken of the Black Community for good or foe, but that is not the entire City of los angeles.
In LA more than a handful of communities made it home where they found opportunities for peace, social and economic growth, and common ground with others.

1-HEALTHY LIVING

The new diet trend, working it off the second half trimming the trio fat

Come the summer and the commitment are serious taking it off from the belly, the waist, and around the arms. For the next six month with some holidays interruptions.

Your body may be in charge of when, where and how you lose fat, but that doesn't mean you can't do something to help things along. Your first step is to focus on losing overall body fat with exercise and a healthy diet. There's no guarantee you'll lose fat from your triceps right away, but allowing your body to respond to your program will tell you what your body is capable of achieving.

Part of that process is strength training for the triceps (and the rest of your body as well). Triceps exercises won't reduce fat there (not specifically, at least), but they do help you build more muscle. More muscle means firmer, stronger triceps and a higher metabolism overall, something that will contribute to overall fat loss.

MBA RESEARCH RESEARCH: LOYOLA UNIVERSITY

Innovation, Resources and Investment Strategies in the US Energy Sector· Abol Jalilvand

and Sung Min Kim analyze and confront the overall insufficiency in innovation and

technological advancement in the US energy sector.

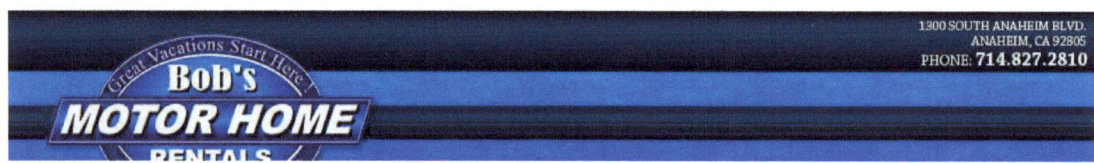
Losing Body Fat

If you want to tone the triceps, focus on:

•Regular cardio exercise in your Target Heart Rate Zone. For fat loss, the general guidelines suggest cardio most days of the week for 30-60 minutes (or working up to that if you're a beginner). More about cardio exercise for weight loss and cardio workouts.

•Strength training for your entire body (triceps included) at least 1-3 non-consecutive days a week. There are endless ways to lift weights, but it's best to start with a simple beginner's program, if you're just getting started. Learn more about strength training for beginners, setting up a complete strength and cardio program, and find a variety of workouts for every fitness level.

•A healthy low-calorie diet. Exercise can help you burn calories, but your diet is where you can really make a difference. A few simple tips to consider:

BEST LODGING DEALS ONLINE

news for traveling: Visit Southern California is a locally owned and operated website with over 10 years in the travel and hospitality industry. All of the listings we offer information for have been using Visit Southern California's marketing services for a number of years. This insures you the user only the best in vacation offers to the Southern California area.

visitsoutherncalifornia.net

You've read that interval training or other cardio exercises can help reduce body fat and that strength training can as well, soit makes sense that including both in your weekly routine would help reduce belly fat even more.

One study confirmed this by following exercisers who did three days of strength training and three days of cardio a week. When comparing this group to the cardio-only group, researchers found that the combined group reduced more belly fat and increased their lean muscle tissue.

•Alternate your workouts: Doing cardio and strength training on different days allows you to focus your energy and attention to each workout.

•Split routines: Another option is to split your workout and do cardio in the morning and strength training later in the day, or vice versa.
•Combine workouts: If you don't have as much time, another option is to do cardio and strength training in the same workout.
When setting up your routine, you may need to experiment to find a schedule that

works for you. Just remember, you don't want to work the same muscles two days in a row, although you can do cardio on consecutive days.

ANAHEIM RESORT AREA EXTENDED STAY

Anaheim Resort, for more details go to the website.

CASTLE INN & SUITES

Anaheim Resort at Disneyland Castle Inn & Suites

Belly Flat, SIXPACK 7, 8: Sixpack to Eightpack by Eddie Elchahed (Jul 15, 2010

On Sale Now, you can take advantage of special offer when you buy from amazon.com

2 -The Source:

Of course it should make a big difference. In this scenario we focus on the source of protein. protein is one vital element of our daily diet. The source of the protein intake is crucial to the development of muscles and a lean body. Protein sources can vary in quality, in quantity or volume, and the price can make a big difference. keeping mind that we are only focusing on the muscles development in relevant to the source of protein intake in our daily diet.

Meat is one source of protein in comparison to penuts as another source, meat is rich in the quantity per volume, but meat include more fat than any other protein source.

According to Dr Mehemet OZ there are two different protein, complete and incomplete.

We need to eat both types found in variety of food,   Proteins are made from 20 amino acids. Complete proteins contain the 9 essential amino acids your body needs to build new proteins. Essential amino acids are ones the body can't produce on its own.
Animal sources of protein tend to be complete. Other protein sources lack one or more of the essential amino acids; these are called incomplete proteins. These include fruits, vegetables, grains and nuts.
Because the body doesn't store amino acids, like it does with fat or carbohydrates, it needs a fresh supply of them every day to make new proteins. Complete and incomplete proteins play an equally important role in this process. The best way to get all the protein you need is to pick from wide and varied sources.

MBA RESEARCH RESEARCH: LOYOLA UNIVERSITY

Innovation, Resources and Investment Strategies in the US Energy Sector· Abol Jalilvand and Sung Min Kim analyze and confront the overall insufficiency in innovation and technological advancement in the US energy sector.

MORTGAGE FINANCING

your home banking needs. Mortgage finance and Refi.

RRMS provides specialty services across the mortgage finance arena. An analysis will be performed on portfolio data to identify the scope of work; strategies will be implemented in accordance with the client's goals and objectives.

rrmsco.com/mortgage-finance/

List of protein sources recommended :

1-Turkey

2-Chicken

3-Fish

4-Tofu

5-Lean Beef

6-Nuts

7-Beans

Beans and nuts are considered either a side dish or munchies, almost always people look at beef as the primary source of protein, and tofu is left for last choice because of the strange sour taste. Beans can be filling like any other dish if was prepared properly from A to Z. and mixed or topped a bowl of rice. the source is important when a person is not getting the average amount of protein needed for either muscles growth or to sustain a healthier and adequate immune system ready to repair and heal any physical threats to the body. Beans sucj as string beans, or any of your favorite can be rolled into a wrape type of sandwich with a mixer of rice and picante salsa, or shredded letuce and diced fresh tomatoes. Nuts are the easy way to accumilate protein throughout the day to mount close to what the body expectation of daily protein intake.

Many argue the accurate amount of protein daily intake is required for the body to progress in building muscles or in supporting the energy output during an average working day. In general the fornula is 2 for 1, for every one pound of body weight 2 grams of protein are necessary for muscles growth and balance energy output. The number become surprising when calculted based on an average man body weight. there suppose to be 300gm of protein needed for a 150 Lbs weight body. many people have gone tothe protein powder to speed up the process and reduce cost of the required protein intake, based on the 2 for 1 formula.

Health.com

3-**Coffee taking over.....regular hot drip or hand craft.**

Coffee was studied by scientists to determine the health effects and the benefits to the body.
Results were outrageous, and here few:

A- Coffee can stimulate your brian cells to not only keep you awake with caffeine ingredients, but to also make you smarter.

Caffeine blocks certain chemicals in the brain leading to stimulate the smarter brain cells or chemicals used for thinking, it open up the channels of those most needed buy blocking others unecessarry cells or chemicals which slow down the flow of the smarter brain cells.

B- The common use of caffeine in medication and diet pills for both control of weight gain, and to boost metabolic ate of burning more calories.

C- Coffee lower the risk of type II Diabetes the most blood disease on the rise n recent years affecting more than 3oo million people. It was proven in a study that caffeine can reduce the risk of diabetes by up to 67%.
people who drink the most coffee during the day are the least to become effected with type II diabetes.

D- Multiple studies results that caffeine can lower the risk liver cancer and liver disorders by as much as 80%.
Coffee contains large amount of nutrients and antioxidants with decent amount of vitamins and minerals which is the largest source in the western diet.

Coffee like any other beverage if it was consume in large quantity with no other alternatives, it become too addictive and harmful to the body. Make sure you stop if you find out that coffee is not your gene type of beverage, and or make adequate adjustment, such as do not add anything to your coffee, or stop drinking at certain amount or at certain time of the day.

Breakdown of Café Types in New York City

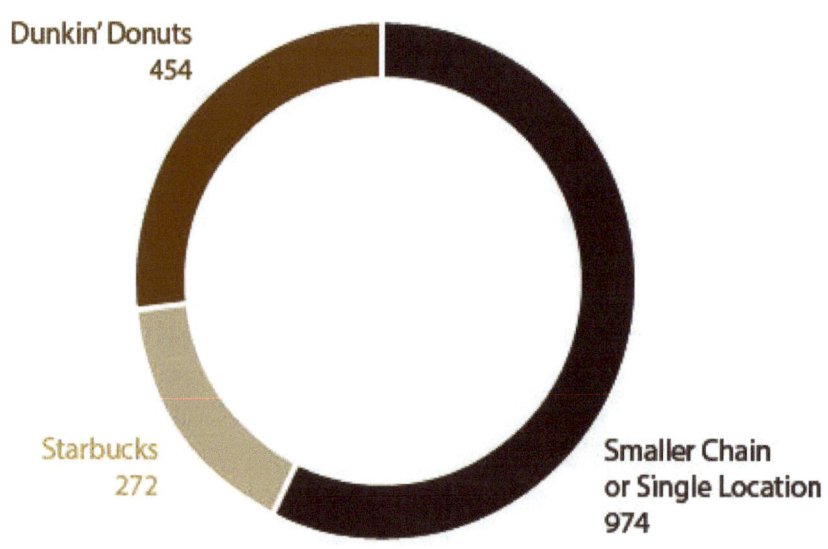

Dunkin' Donuts
454

Starbucks
272

Smaller Chain
or Single Location
974

Source: Restaurant Inspection Results, New York City Department of Health and Mental Hygiene, January 2013

4 It i a new world

IN A PERFECT WORLD EVERYTHING NOT POSSIBLE

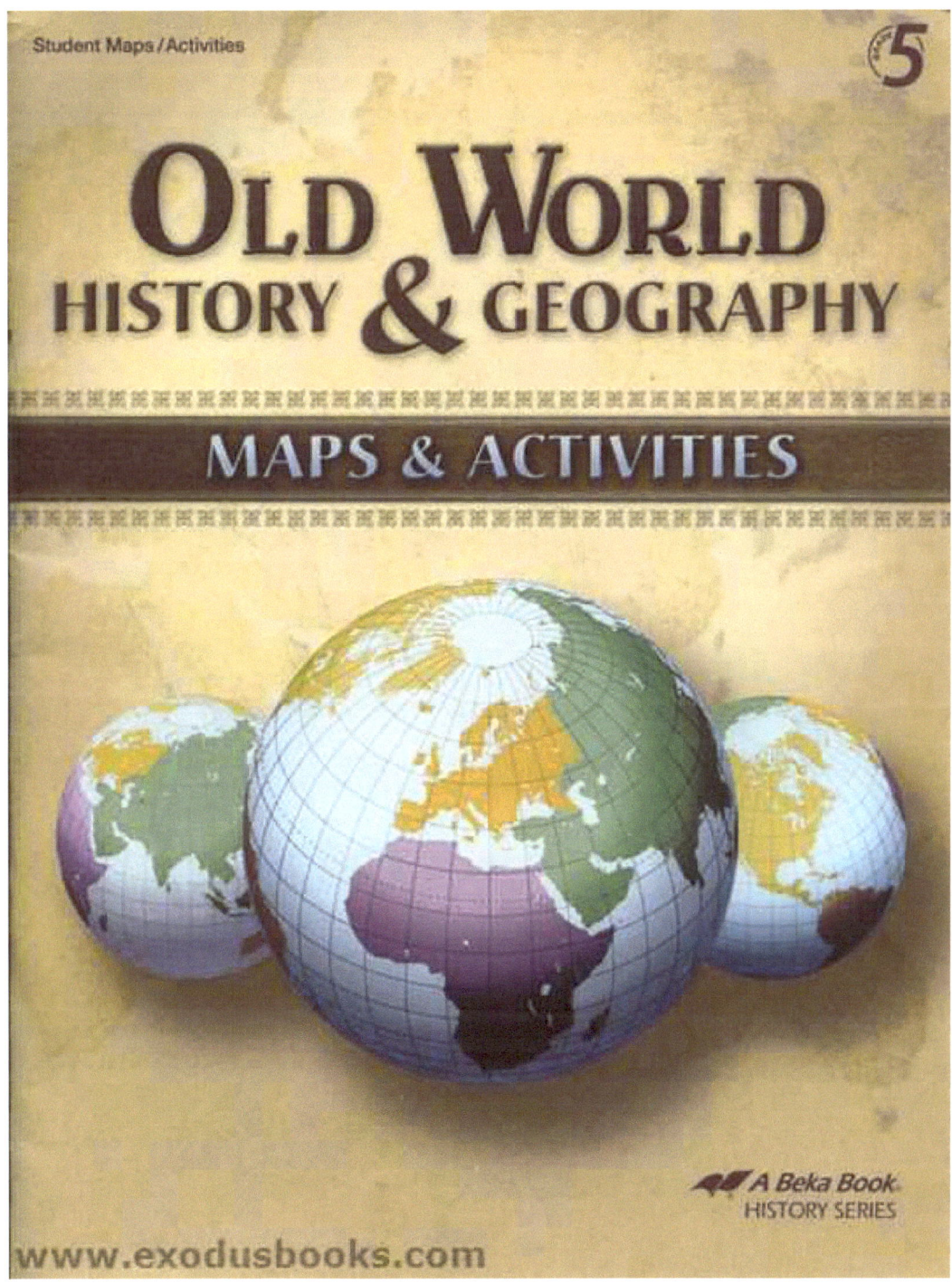

Old World Map…1200 AD- 1400 AD

In the world where all the holly books were the leading message from God. Profits, and religion scientists wrote books on everything to prove to the common man that wisdom is in the hands of the creator God. The stars and how the sun and the moon circulate in the twilight zone, the rain,and any odd theory which relevant was quoted by philosophers and scientists to be translated to all languages and taught in schools everywhere so that everyone will take notice and have common knowledge.

This was 1300 years after discovery, or about 1400 years from discovery.Kingdom came and gone with truly perfect civilization with all the tools to predict, analyse, and further more to check and balance on any results for accuracy.

You might be able to do almost everything back in the old world before the second discovery,or let us call it as such because it is extremely parallel to the center point of the

original. It is no secret about the discovery of the new world after all of that believing that

was the "stairway to heaven". People pointed their fingers in that direction where the sun

set and the sun rose again as it was the place for the heavens. The end of man final

address.

How did the religious super powers confronted the new discovery of the Americas?.it was

the best thing came along to escape the religion aggression among catholic and protestant

in Europe. There was no time to argue or to make corrections.

Among the itemized agenda for the study funding for Columbus was to convert the

natives to Christianity, beside the number one item and down the list of finding new trade

routes beside Africa, and China.

In a summary, no one wanted to confront the truth about the accurate geography

according to the religious scholars and to argue against the royals and their explorers was

forbidden.The royals carried spiritual ties with God. it was believed that taking a shower

or a bath back then will reduce the spiritual layers from the body. Royals in Europe and

many of their followers took a bath on a monthly basis.

Finally, the new world discovery change everything in the old books of geography, history,

and science, so did many religious books, and all of the those who pursuit the idea that the

world was square, and that where the sun set,it was the end. The possibility of preaching

the world finest religions, and to lead people to believe that this is the final destination was

ommited due to the legal requirement,

.Eddie Elchahed , Publisher, Editor.07/20/13. 2:35 PM..(I was told by a common man,

hard-working man, from before the sun rise until after it set, "The Native Indians had it

all figured out, fish and hunt", he was paying for his groceries at a Wall Mart cashier

stand, i was next. The groceries were $82 and change. There was fish, beef, and some chicken.and other items.

Source: News U.S.Journal at nusjournal.com

5__ Becoming taller natural

Becoming taller natural is making adjustments in areas of your body which can eliminate for example the down fall of the shoulder s or the arching of the back.

Exercising the Core area of the body can lead to an increase in body heights.

Loosing belly fat and flating the abdominal wall will resolve in at least couple of inches increase in heights.

exercise the upper body using pull ups, hanging, toe touch exercise, cobra, bow down, pelvic shift, and leg stretch.

Exercise and Diet are the best to grow taller naturally.

HOW YOU CAN
GROW TALLER
AT ANY AGE!

Forward
Head

Flat
Back ck

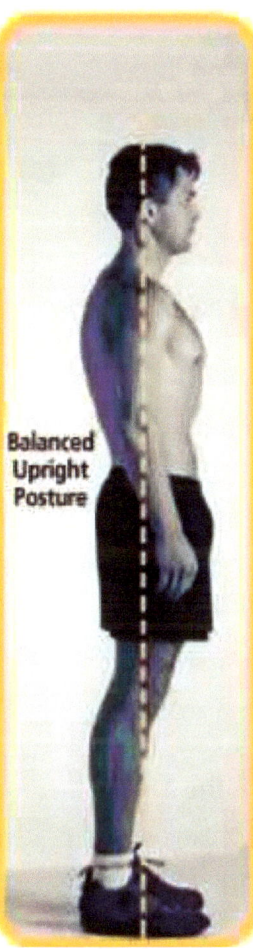

Balanced
Upright
Posture

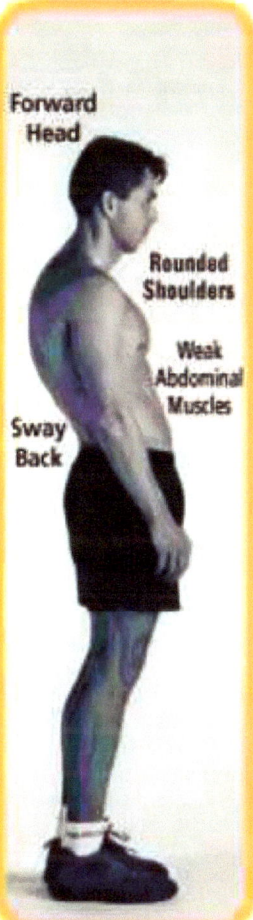

Forward
Head

Rounded
Shoulders

Weak
Abdominal
Muscles

Sway
Back

Do you know 94% women say that **HEIGHT** is the **MOST attractive feature** of man?

Research proved that taller guys **make more money** AND enjoy happier life than shorter guys

Models, Wrestlers, NBA Players are all taller in their height

It does matter either you are man or woman you agree with me height is the most important factor to get attraction from opposite sex and get dream job

Exactly 8 years ago…

Darwin Smith was also same like you… he was 5ft 8" (176 cm) BUT… still want to grow taller WHY?

BECAUSE…

His favorite wrestler **POWERHOUSE** in this industry Goldberg is above 6 ft and…

Almost every legend superstar wrestlers are above 6ft (182 cm)

The Rock, Stone Cold, Hulk Hogan, Undertaker, Big Show are just few of them

He knew if he wants to get same crazy fan followers he has to reach above 6ft

He tried lots and lots of diet, creams, HGH pills, taller shoes but nothing works… He wants PERMANENT height

Source: Secrets research.

It is by e-mail but you can include your phone number in the product disription if you wish for people to call you.

Connections magazine is member of we connect 2 network. Online publishing,

multi-media public relation,

news monitoring, and communities promotions. weconnect2.com, policewitoutborders.com, News U.S.Journal, and now Connections magazine is the new addition to the network. For your advertising needs, please visit weconnect2.com at Custom Advertising Zone.

Southern California This Weekend

****SOUTHERN CALIFORNIA THIS WEEKEND******
PLACES AND THINGS TO DO WE RECOMMEND IN SOUTHERN
CALIFORNIA. BASED ON OUR EXPERIENCE, REFERENCE BY
TRUSTED SOURCE, AND GOOD REPORT FROMOUR ASSOCIATES.
*******************SOUTHERN CALIFORNIA THIS
WEEKEND********************************

Downtown Fullerton is one of the fun places to visit on the weekend, college town, 5 miles North of Anaheim Disney, and easy access by all means of transportation. It is for everyone..Kids,Families, students, and those who are looking for great experience, dinning, music, and people watching.

Fullerton got it. Merchants and residents have worked hard throughout the years to built a solid community with good image and reformed trust in the public safety local agencies. Here you will relive many of experiences of my teen and young adulthood, at Tuscany or Florence, and out to the other side by the OCTA bus station depot is Sidebar special effect, the patio live band.

Come and detail the rest of the experience, walk around this small but mystique fun downtown, use the bus, cab, the train or have friend drive for few Bucs, hit that 2 in one stone,so you can have a great time without the worries of the possibility to DUI, make sure for an alternative to keep some cabs phone numbers on you. friends do not let friends drive

intoxicated..

Daily Hot topic. at weconnect2.com

Everyday most relevant article, press release, and topic. Most important to our daily living. Best ten is the ranking of the content or subject the article or press release bring to us as readers and audience.

HOT TOPIC

These are examples you can find more at the web.

-When is the right time to be an entrepreneur and or open for business?
-Money Trouble? 14 Depression-Fighting Tips

-A Bull in Stocks, but a Bear for Free Speech

-Heat Exhaustion and Heat Stroke

-**Boy awarded $6.9 million: The Los Angeles school district must pay $6.9 million to a boy sexually molested by his elementary school teacher, says a jury. The ruling says the school district is liable for the acts of Forrest Stobbe who was a teacher at Queen Anne Elementary School.**

Advertising Page

proper attire

Fashion statement for everyone. make it sound.

Shop online at weconnect2.com

Photography.

Photography at National University

Costa Mesa, Ca Campus.

For all your advertising needs, visit weconnect2.com Custom Advertising Zone.